I0796515

# ISABEL LÓPEZ-QUESADA

# Isabel López-Quesada
## AT HOME

PHOTOGRAPHS BY
MIGUEL FLORES-VIANNA

FOREWORD BY AMY ASTLEY

VENDOME
NEW YORK · LONDON

# CONTENTS

Biarritz
112
GRACIAS
239

# FOREWORD AMY ASTLEY

In the luscious pages of her first book, Isabel López-Quesada offers lessons in living that resonate and inspire just as much as her aesthetic lessons. The three personal residences she shares—her family's main home in Madrid and their two holiday houses in Biarritz—are not overtly or self-consciously "decorated"; there are neither "statement" pieces nor the design and art world trophies that have become de rigueur in so many fashionable interiors.

Rather, López-Quesada's quiet, sensuous spaces emphasize her reverence for life's simple pleasures—gardens, trees, flowers, sunlight, fountains, books, a cozy reading nook, a big claw-foot tub. She rejects the gratuitously pricey or the frankly pretentious in favor of humble domestic materials like antique linens, aged stone floors, porcelain, wicker baskets, quilts, and weathered family heirlooms. The fact that López-Quesada has decided to feature her own homes instead of those created for clients allows the reader to profoundly grasp the personal philosophy that underscores her signature design vision.

I know López-Quesada as an internationally acclaimed interior designer, but now also see her, unexpectedly, as a charmingly low-key domestic goddess, at once glamorous, sophisticated, and salt of the earth. She shows us her lovingly stocked linen closets; her—sigh—ironing room; the kitchen patio where she grows cooking herbs; cupboards and armoires groaning with stacks of pottery, silverware, goblets, and glasses. (Indeed, she lays many a pretty table in this book.) She values her kitchens for their utility more than their looks, especially calling out such homey details as double refrigerators for "when we have a full house" and an antique marble sink ideal for both flower arranging and dog washing.

Perhaps López-Quesada's greatest joy and passion is nature. With endearing understatement and modesty, she describes the spectacular space she has created in Madrid as "a house in a garden"—emphasis firmly on the garden. In these homes, enormous windows and French doors open onto carefully considered outdoor spaces that López-Quesda's legendary landscape designer Fernando Caruncho describes as "additional rooms." Indoors, the rooms themselves brim with glorious flowers, usually arranged by López-Quesada herself. In Biarritz, clearly her happy place, she even has a flower atelier in which she has installed two authentic florist's work tables—on wheels!—to aid in her favorite pastime.

These rooms are thoughtfully designed for the enjoyment of her children, her husband, her guests, and, of course, herself. They are rooms conceived to cocoon loved ones and visitors, rather than to impress or intimidate. They are rooms full of love and joy.

López-Quesada's is a life well—and beautifully—lived. And if we never have the good fortune to land an invitation to one of her houses, we do have this book, welcoming us into an enchanted world where family and nature reign supreme, as it should be.

# INTRODUCTION

I had been toying with the idea of a book about my work for some time–a summary of my career, featuring my best projects in Spain and around the world, my travels across half the globe in search of fabrics, spaces, and inspiration. Yet, during my first meeting with Mark Magowan, publisher of Vendome Press, our conversation kept returning to the three houses I've built for my family and myself. To Mark it was obvious: Why not start with a book about my own homes? Don't they best capture what defines and explains me? And not only my work as an interior designer but also my instinct, my taste, my life? An Argentine friend of mine often says that homes are like romances. So in these pages, and through the lens of Miguel Flores-Viana's unique and sophisticated eye, I present you with my three great loves, my three corners of heaven on earth.

This year I celebrated thirty-five years in the business. I opened my first studio when I was twenty years old. Teaming up with a friend, I found a small place on the calle de Montesquinza in Madrid, and we threw ourselves into our work with a passion, taking on anything and everything–no job was too small or unimportant. From day one, I had no doubt that this was my calling. In fact, I had known it since I was thirteen. I remember the exact moment it happened: my mother wanted to change the look of the hall in our house and she asked us who wanted to go with her to choose new fabrics. All my sisters fled, but I eagerly agreed to accompany her. By the time we returned home, I knew: I was going to be a decorator. I studied at the Escuela de Artes Decorativas, a private college next to the Puerta de Alcalá, in the center of Madrid, but even then I was a free spirit. I was never the perfect student and prefer to think of myself as self-taught.

But I did have role models; the two people who influenced me the most were my maternal grandmother and my mother. If I have a gift or talent, I owe it to them. Like my mother, my grandmother Isabel was beautiful and elegant, with a keen aesthetic sense. When the Spanish Civil War ended, my grandparents and their four daughters went to live in Argentina, escaping the harsh conditions in postwar Spain. They enjoyed a joyful, light-filled life there and brought that atmosphere back with them years later when they returned to their house in Madrid. My grandmother decorated it with French moldings, velvet, colorful damasks, and marvelous Zuber scenic wallpapers, including Isola Bella. My mother inherited her mother's incredible eye and sophisticated taste, which she in turn passed on to her daughters. As huge as their influence was, I would be remiss not to mention the impact that my father has had

**Above:** The old wax factory in Madrid, as it looked when I first saw it in 1999.

on me. Raised in an entrepreneurial family involved in banking and the Caterpillar company, he has whimsically eccentric taste and is an open-minded, optimistic, sporty man. His playful yet pragmatic character, honed during his years as a student in the United States, instilled in me an unprejudiced, determined, and positive attitude toward work and life.

And now back to the matter at hand: my three homes. My three adventures. The first, a former wax factory, built in 1931, is in Madrid. The second is a former pheasant farm near Biarritz, in the south of France. And the third is a former *gallinero* (henhouse) on the same farm. Three structures that had a history before they became my homes. Transforming them was a personal effort that illustrates something crucial about me: I follow my impulses, I fall in love with places that appear unexpectedly, hold on to them fast, and never let go. Where others saw only hopeless ruins, I saw new paths. To accompany me on these paths, I found two friends and fellow travelers, the architect Pablo Carvajal, who designed the house in Madrid with me, and Fernando Caruncho, whose poetic hand is felt in all the gardens in this book, which we designed together.

**Opposite, clockwise from top left:** My grandmother Isabel, Condesa de Ulloa de Monterrey, painted by Luis Mosquera; my grandmothers, Lola and Isabel, with my mother; my mother and I at a wedding; my children, Álvaro, Claudia, and Isabel, with our dog Pepito; me, dressed as a flamenco dancer; me, in the studio; my parents, Jaime and Loreto, in my grandmother's house, early 1960s; six of us with our dog Blue; my grandmother Isabel and me; my mother; background: detail of Isola Bella, one of the Zuber wallpapers that hung in my grandmother's home.

The old wax factory, my family's home for the last fifteen years, consisted of the house in which the factory owners lived, two storehouses, and two courtyards, which allowed me to build an oasis in the middle of the city. I remember showing Álvaro, my husband, photographs of the factory and his initial disbelief in what I wanted to do. He had faith, however, and three years later we had our new house, which was undoubtedly the greatest before-and-after transformation of my career. The greenery, coolness, and water features of the courtyards are all in stark contrast to arid Madrid. Like the other houses in this book, it was conceived slowly, without rushing, over time. That is the advantage of doing your own house; you can make decisions calmly, seeing what works and what doesn't, observing how the light comes in and changes throughout the day. I like a simple layout; I am classical, yet my pragmatic side also makes me modern. A real house is a comfortable house, made to be lived in, used, and enjoyed. This means getting rid of extraneous elements. Neither minimalist nor maximalist, I suppose I belong in some undefined category in between.

Nothing makes me happier than transforming a dilapidated space into something new and different, and once inside, experiencing its transformation, which is also my own. In my understanding of decoration, nothing remains the same forever. Decoration is a living thing. The passing of time, the play of textures and colors, the mix of furnishings, fresh flowers—perhaps these are the only things that never change in the way I see a space.

I always wanted to have a farm, and after many years vacationing in the south of France, I found a farmhouse on the outskirts of Biarritz. It is the home where I am certain I will retire, when the time comes. A family house, it is full of cool, spacious rooms and small details: lots of rustic wood, predominantly white walls, and old family portraits, casually hung on the walls. It is a gathering point during vacations, a place that brings us together. Just as in the Madrid house, my three children have a world of their own in this house, yet it is an open world, always in touch with ours. Their rooms reflect their different personalities and interests. To see them growing up in spaces they enjoy and have made their own is a gift for both them and me.

Opposite, clockwise from top left: Hôtel du Palais, Biarritz; my mother with the twins, Inés and Sofía; the first four girls: Loreto, me, Elena, and María; my husband, Álvaro Llanza, Marques del Valle de Oaxaca, me, and our children, Claudia, Isabel, and Álvaro, at the beach in Biarritz; La Grande Plage, Biarritz; the first six of us: Jaime, María, Elena, me, Loreto, and Carmen, the baby in my arms; my grandparents Miguel and Isabel Sanchiz, Condes de Ulloa de Monterrey, in Punta del Este, Uruguay.

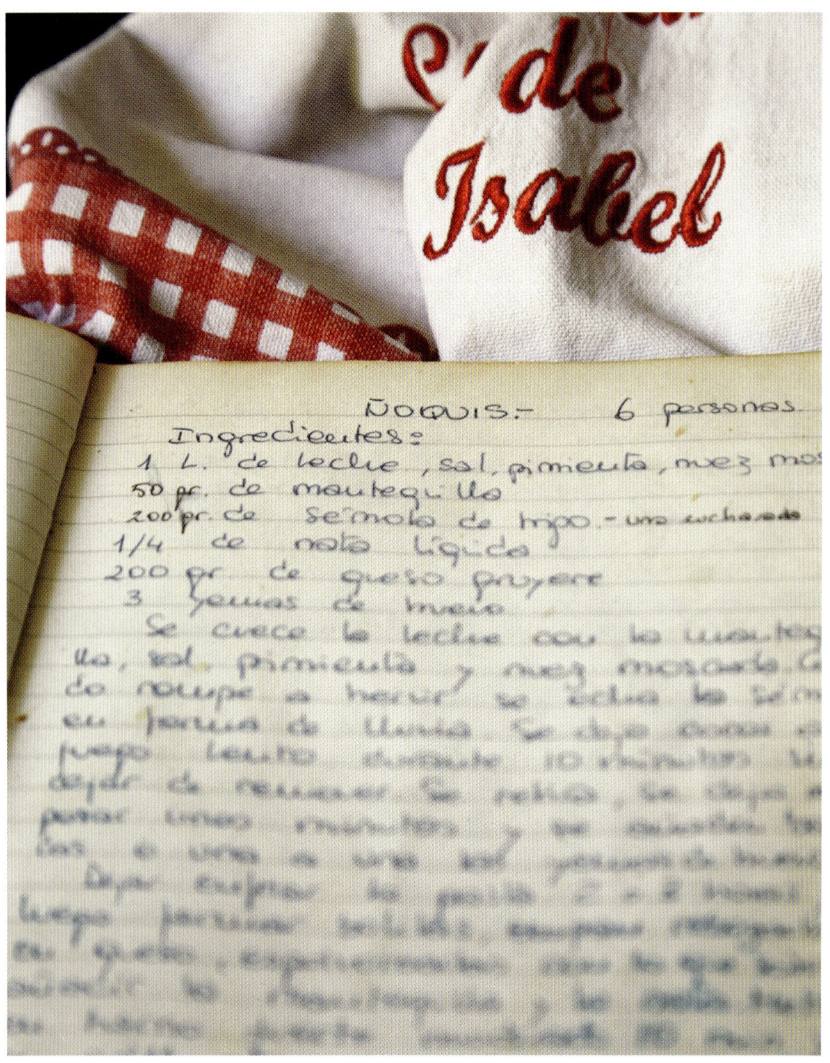
de
Isabel
ÑOQUIS.- 6 personas
Ingredientes:
1 L. de leche, sal, pimienta, nuez mos
50 gr. de mantequilla
200 gr. de sémola de trigo.-
1/4 de nata líquida
200 gr. de queso gruyere
3 yemas de huevo

The farm came with a small surprise. The main building was surrounded by seven small henhouses, including a special one that was larger than the others, measuring 300 square meters (more than 3,000 square feet), and ideally oriented toward the south, facing La Rhune, the highest peak in the Labourd region, a summit brimming with folklore and legends. Instead of demolishing the ramshackle structure, I decided to transform it into a cabin, using all the old, spare, leftover stuff I came across. I keep everything because I believe everything finds its place. All the extra doors and windows from the main house ended up in the cabin. I even put my son to work as a carpenter during the summer! Half play, half experiment. I covered the living room walls with the corrugated-metal plates that had clad the exterior of the *gallinero*. If I do say so myself, it ended up being something quite special. A very inexpensive, sturdy building, comfortable both in winter and in summer. If you ask my kids, they'll tell you it's their favorite house. And they're not the only ones; many others think the cabin is my most important work, and they may be right. In any case, it was the craziest, most improvised project of my career.

I am lucky to work in a field that I thoroughly enjoy. It is a profession that is learned on the job, but decorating a house also incorporates one's life and experiences. The rigors of the job go hand in hand with one's impulses and intuitions. The houses I design combine the two. There are echoes in all of them of my grandmother Isabel, my childhood, and even the gnocchi recipe that my grandmother brought back from Argentina and that was served at every family gathering, always smothered in cream and cheese. It is the aroma of the three adventures in this book.

Opposite: My grandmother Isabel's gnocchi recipe, which we serve at every family gathering.

# Madrid

When I found the old wax factory, with its little house and two storehouses, I knew it was meant for me. I always say I knew immediately, although it was all thanks to my husband, who, without any professional expertise, trusted my vision implicitly. I saw the house when I was thirty-seven years old and had three children, aged ten, eight, and six. I was working constantly, so to be with them, I needed a studio close to home, and the wax factory offered the perfect solution to bring work and family together. We bought it in 2000. The next year was spent setting up the studio, and by 2003 we were living in the house. The people who worked with me on the project were the architect Pablo Carvajal and the landscape designer Fernando Caruncho. We have been a great team ever since. Our motto is: "Keep it simple, keep it real, keep it honest."

The design of the house was informed by a basic idea: it would be timeless and universal. Pablo had renovated an old dry cleaning establishment and the dry cleaner's house, and he was perfect for this project. The moment he saw the place, he knew it was worth it. "It's a gem," he told me. For the courtyards, I turned to Fernando, a childhood friend whose creativity was crucial to achieve what I wanted. For the three of us, what was most important was to unite the architecture of the house with the landscaping of the courtyards. As Fernando said, "This is a house in a garden and the three of us share a common passion–gardens." When Fernando explains his approach to garden design, he speaks of the importance of light: "The goal is light, to capture what they call the 'mood' of light. It's not something mystical; it's physics. A way of handling light that makes everything resonate and work, that makes the vibrating light from outside flood into the house." I could not have said it any better. There is something intangible about the house that is difficult to describe, but it has something to do with the luminous feeling coming from outside that suffuses and unifies every room.

East elevation

West elevation

# Public Rooms

## Entrance Hall

The hall is a meeting point and the first impression you receive. It is important that this first impression be direct and somehow capture the essence of the house. I like spacious, empty, clean entrances. Located at the center of the residence, the hall connects the two old storehouses. On entering, one immediately senses the clear, simple layout, providing access to the entire house and the courtyards.

The decoration of the hall is sparse, allowing the configuration of the floor–a geometric pattern of two kinds of Spanish stone and a Belgian one, in black, beige, and gray–to dominate. The only other decorative feature is the eighteenth-century French stripped-oak door inset with mirrors instead of glass panes. The staircase is barely perceptible, almost like a line drawn on the wall. To the right, beyond the oak door is the comfy lounge with its library, linen sofa, and magnificent fireplace. To the left is the living room.

## Living Room

The living room is square-shaped, with four pairs of French doors opening out onto the two courtyards. There are no curtains because the French doors frame a live painting that changes throughout the day and the year. The living room enjoys direct sunlight from early morning to midday. The furniture is my attempt at a blend of styles, quite distinct and bold. An eighteenth-century French Louis XVI fireplace dominates one of the main seating areas of the room.

The color scheme of the space is quite neutral–beige and white. Colors are relegated to the details: the Murano glass; the artwork, including a photograph by Jose Dávila, two beeswax panels by José María Sicilia, a number of resin-based works by Dustin Yellin, a drawing by Antonio Saura, a sculpture by Mayte Alonso; and my turtles, which are everywhere. I've been collecting antique turtles for years; perhaps I love them so much because turtles move around with their homes on their backs! Of course, I'm not that slow! I adore tortoiseshell, and turtles follow me wherever I go.

FRANCIS BACON
Chanel
CUBISM
THE LEONARD A. LAUDER COLLECTION
DAMIEN HIRST
SUNNYLANDS

Josef Albers

LAS RAZAS HUMANAS
HISTORIA NATURAL
HISTORIA DE ESPAÑA
GEOGRAFIA UNIVERSAL
GEOGRAFIA DE ESPAÑA
HISTORIA UNIVERSAL
ZOOLOGIA
BOTANICA
INSTITUTO GALLACH

FRANCIS BACON
Joaquín Sorolla
Chanel
DAMIEN HIRST
MUSEO ARCHEOLOGICO NAZIONALE NAPOLI
SUNNYLANDS

Josef Albers

El retrato español
DEL GRECO A PICASSO
PENNOYER KIDDER
A HOUSE IN THE COUNTRY

## Dining Room

As in so many Spanish homes, the dining room is the gathering place for family and friends. Culturally, we love to eat and we enjoy a well-set table. I have a particular weakness for dinnerware, which I feel is one of the most appealing elements of a house. Over the years, I have inherited and bought genuine wonders, ranging from nineteenth-century English treasures to a 1990s colored-glass service by fashion designer Sybilla, that I love to combine. Flower arrangements, candleholders, antique napkins . . . Conventional table settings bore me, and I set my table differently every time, mixing better pieces with less important ones.

The dining room is so important to me that I have two tables, which gives me a lot of flexibility and undermines the idea of a dining room as a rigid, static space. The smaller table feels as if it is situated in a greenhouse; having lunch or an afternoon snack surrounded by light and flowers is always a pleasure. The larger one is set along a wall covered in a black-striped fabric hung with a series of drawings by Jorge Méndez Blake–seventeen visual poems that keep us company during our lengthy after-dinner conversations.

EL VIAJERO
DISEÑO DE JARDINES

## Library

The lounge, or library, is one of the house's most-used rooms. We spend hours here chatting, reading, watching films. The space envelops you. There's the marvelous fireplace that we bought in Poitiers, near Paris, on an unbearably cold day. The Noir Belge floor is a beauty, and both the classic Eames Lounge Chair and the linen sofa invite you to enter, get comfy, and enjoy. Like the rest of the house, the palette is beige and gray, with color provided by the artwork, such as the striking orange circle, an Italian lithograph from the 1960s, on the mantelpiece. The photograph above the sofa, by the Madrid-born photographer Juan de Sande, is from a series of old industrial buildings. I designed the glass-topped, matte-finished-steel side tables, and the two stone lamps are finials from a garden balustrade. From the sofa, one can contemplate the sights and sounds of the large courtyard: the sun, the patter of the rain falling into the pool, the rustling of the bamboo. For many reasons, the library is a special place.

EL TALISMAN
LES KILIMS

TASCHEN
Jaime Parladé

GMAT
PRACTICAS DE ANALISIS DE BALANCES
análisis de balances
MARIO PUZO LOS BORGIA
GARY JENNINGS SANGRE AZTECA
THE DECISIVE BATTLES OF THE WESTERN WORLD
JESÚS CACHO
CASIMIRO GARCÍA-ABADILLO
LUIS HERRERO CONDE, EL ÁNGEL CAÍDO
Christopher Knight y Robert Lomas
LO QUE MÁS NOS IMPORTABA
John Grisham LA TAPADERA
John Grisham EL CLIENTE
ERA MEDIANOCHE EN BHOPAL
BAUMANN

EL REAL CLUB DE LA
PUERTA DE HIERRO
EL REAL CLUB DE LA
ALTAREJOS UN JARDÍN EN LA DEHESA Carlos March EDICIONES EL VISO
1947-1968

## Kitchen

The kitchen, located off the larger of the courtyards, is a place of constant activity and foot traffic. All white and stainless steel, on the one hand it serves as a kitchen-lab, functional and modern, and on the other it is a nexus of family life and flux. This is where our dog, a Labrador named Olivia, has her bed. The kitchen's warmth and my personality are found in the antique marble sink (where we wash Olivia and I arrange my flowers!), my endless vase collection, an old table surrounded by Eames armchairs for Vitra, and a work by Yuri Masnyj, a still life with nods to historical avant-garde movements that has found its place in this room, so central to the day-to-day life of the house.

## Service Rooms

I have a very special relationship with textiles. They have great importance to me. Stamped, plain, embroidered, striped, geometric, and especially anything with flowers, always lots of flowers. Linen, cotton, used, inherited . . . The linen closet itself, filled with tablecloths, sheets, pillowcases, and napkins, large and embroidered, is lined with remnants from my studio. It is a special cupboard; each shelf holds a different fabric. The linens are very important in this house, and that is why the ironing room, very traditional in Spain, is almost a place of worship, a symbol of my love of fabrics and their freshness.

NEUTREX

# Private Rooms

## Master Bedroom

Of the two storehouses we renovated, the more square one became the small master suite, quite bare despite the decorative elements. The bedroom has a fireplace that I bought in Versailles, an oak four-poster bed, always dressed in linens and cottons, many of them vintage, and two mirrored nightstands. One of my favorite pieces is the eighteenth-century Swedish polychromatic table with the tiled top at the foot of the bed. The drawing above the fireplace is Blaze Lamper's *Weeping Tree*. The room may appear feminine–flowers everywhere!–but it also has a masculine touch, thanks to the *capriccios*, eighteenth-century Italian landscapes, that reflect Álvaro's passion for Italy.

VELÁZQUEZ
THE TIMES Atlas of WORLD HISTORY

KEN FOLLETT
FALL OF GIANTS

## Dressing Rooms

We have two connecting dressing rooms, one of which, my husband's, leads to the bathroom. His dressing room is an assemblage of his interests, particularly his passion for golf. All his trophies are displayed in an English cabinet. Mine is a feminine fantasy where I could spend hours and hours. Here I have my dressing table, my chaise longue, and the wardrobes with French moldings that I retrieved from my grandmother's house. Everything stimulates my senses: the jewelry cases, the clothes, my passion for patterns and prints, the perfumes, the creams . . . And it is all on display. These are my memories, my world. I am happy here and, as you might have guessed, it's also my daughters' favorite place!

Ilmos. Sres. Marqueses del Valle de Oaxa
Madrid
España
CORREOS
Franqueo Pagado en Oficina

JO MALONE

## Master Bathroom

My clients often ask me for individual bathrooms, but my husband and I have shared a bathroom since we were married. This one receives the morning sun, and the tub, situated beneath a large window covered in jasmine that flowers in May, is an indulgence I allowed myself when I turned forty. The floor is French, the marble lining the shower is Italian, there are two washbasins, and I finished the shade covering the window with the trim from an old sheet I found in el Rastro, Madrid's most atmospheric open-air Sunday flea market.

Ysabel Herrero.

## Children's Bedrooms

My three children's bedrooms, like the rest of the house, look out on the courtyards. When my older daughter, Claudia, became independent, I turned the two girls' rooms into one large one, and now my younger daughter, Isabel, has a great space all to herself. A large bed faces the two windows. Just as my husband and I decorated our private space according to our taste, our children have created their own worlds in their rooms, and the details define them more than me. They have their own personalities, and I like it that way. Yet their rooms are unified with the rest of the house by the light and greenery that come through the windows.

# Courtyards

Landscape designer Fernando Caruncho's poetic hand has touched all my houses. In the Madrid house, as he himself explains, "The courtyards are essentially two additional rooms." Madrid is a city with a dry climate, yet we have created a small urban oasis that protects us from the summer's overwhelming heat and changes throughout the rest of the year. The courtyard gardens generate the cool temperature, the greenery, and the light that floods in through all the doors and windows. For the most part, they are very simple and unadorned, underscoring the message that house and garden are one.

I have said it before and I'll say it again: this is a house in a garden. It is impossible to fully appreciate the splendor of these courtyards without experiencing them. From April to June, everything flowers. The jasmine, the roses, the linden tree, the four chestnut trees . . . When in bloom, they take over the space and create an incredible little forest. Fernando always says that a tree lends veracity to a house, and that is what the linden and chestnut trees do. Surrounding the house with bamboo was another of Fernando's inspired ideas. It grows fast, stays green all year round, and shields us completely from the neighboring houses. The moment spring arrives, we open up the doors and windows, move from room to room through the courtyards, and begin to have lunch and dinner outdoors. The trees provide shade–the linden tree in one courtyard, the chestnut trees in the other–and everywhere, the soothing sound of water can be heard.

There is no need to explain the relaxing quality of the sound of water. In the courtyards, it infuses the whole space with a sensorial harmony. Spain has a rich tradition of incorporating water features–fountains, wells, and pools–into house and garden design. In my house, water is present in different forms, including the long fountain that runs the length of one of the courtyards, and the pool, whose oxidized bottom offers a stunningly beautiful and harmonious reflection of colors. "The long fountain highlights the entrance courtyard," says the architect, Pablo Carvajal. "Visually, it leads the eye to the chestnut tree at the back, and it creates an almost imperceptible connection to the living room," Fernando Caruncho adds.

When the heat sets in, we enjoy swimming outdoors. In the evenings, we have dinner alfresco, amid the scents and sounds of the garden. Like the furniture inside, the garden furniture is a combination of styles and materials: iron, wicker, wood. The pieces are practical and durable, covered in fabrics, cushions, and tablecloths of diverse origins and colors. Water, flowers, and fabrics–what more can one ask for? A visual delight. A sensory feast resulting from precise and delicate teamwork. "It's all intuitive," Fernando says. "One works with one's own knowledge and a lot of intuition."

# Studio

The studio was originally the two-story house in which the owners of the wax factory lived. The ground floor is now the showroom, and the studio itself occupies the second floor. My team consists of eleven people. Working here, with so much light and so little noise, surrounded by courtyards, is a delight. My office is full of books, plans, and fabric samples. It is an open space that everyone uses. The table, more than three meters long, is great for anything, a place for meetings and gatherings. Beside it is a smaller one, an Italian engineer's drafting table that I turned into a collage of photographs, mementos, and just things that I like and enjoy looking at. The studio's architecture, very different from that of the house, dates to 1931 and is in the style of old Madrid summer houses. When we renovated it, I took down all the partition walls and drop ceilings to expose the original wood ceiling. We painted it white, gaining even more light, air, and space—three elements essential to my daily life.

# Biarritz

I had dreamed of a farm for a long time. I had seen Sydney Pollack's *Out of Africa*, based on Isak Dinesen's memoirs of her life in Kenya, and had fantasized about having a house like hers on the outskirts of Nairobi. Africa, of course, was too distant a dream, but the south of France, where my husband's family has always vacationed, seemed a more likely place for my dream to be fulfilled. Two years after we finished our house in Madrid, an opportunity in Biarritz arose: a pheasant farm–La Faisanderie–built on land with great views.

When I began looking for a place, I asked Fernando Caruncho, who would later be in charge of designing the garden and the surrounding landscape, what I should focus on in my search for land in the countryside, and he said something I felt was quite enigmatic, although I took it to heart and have never forgotten it: "What you should look for is land with a lot of sky." I had asked about the features of a good piece of land and he told me to look at the sky! The truth is that the location of the house, Arcangues (Arrangoitze in Basque), means "on the top of the hill." In the past it was an oak forest, and in fact the terrain is rather hilly. And yes, there was sky and light everywhere.

The house was in really bad shape and had an annex that blocked the best view. However, I was not in a rush to change it. Before deciding what to do, I painted it white and fixed it up just enough to live in it during the first summer with my family so I could figure out what needed to be done. Spending that summer in the house, with one bathroom for everyone and the bare necessities, proved to be not only an incredibly fun experience but also essential for getting to know the virtues and flaws of the site. The light, the views, everything was important, and that summer in the house helped me get the renovation just right.

We enjoy this house all year long, and not a month goes by without a visit, except perhaps February, when it's usually too cold and inhospitable. In any case, I never stop feeling that someday it will become my primary residence, a house conceived to be enjoyed together with my children and grandchildren. A twenty-first-century farm.

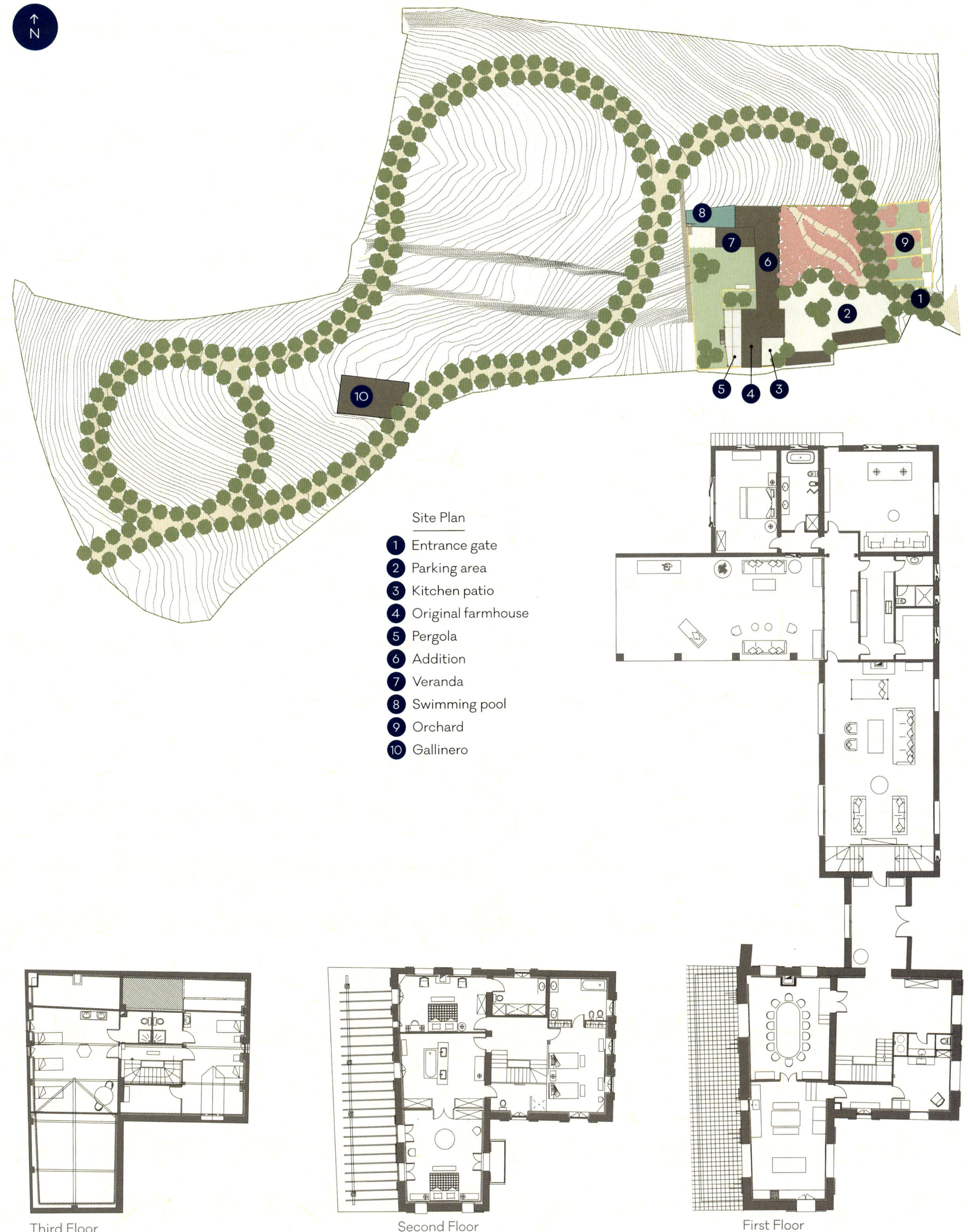
N
1
2
3
4
5
6
7
8
9
10
Site Plan
1 Entrance gate
2 Parking area
3 Kitchen patio
4 Original farmhouse
5 Pergola
6 Addition
7 Veranda
8 Swimming pool
9 Orchard
10 Gallinero
Third Floor
Second Floor
First Floor

# Public Rooms

It took us three years to rebuild and renovate the Biarritz house, including the cabin–or *gallinero* (henhouse)–and the garden. We proceeded incrementally, again without rushing. In the main house, we demolished what we thought was wrong and we devised an addition that would allow us to extend to the north and retreat from the village road.

We built the one-floor addition six meters (twenty feet) away from the original nineteenth-century house and connected it to the old building via a hall. I preserved the character of the old house–the beams and the walls, including some of the original paint, which I left as "frescoes." Essentially, I integrated some of the house's scars and wounds to give it personality. My idea was for everything to be simple and natural, retaining the flavor of the past. We accented the new building with antique architectural elements and materials salvaged from other houses, like doors found in Navarre and terra-cotta tiles from France for the hall floor. With just a few details, we managed to give a unified feel to the whole house; both the old and the new buildings appear to be from the same period.

2
2

## Entrance Hall

One of the challenges of this house was to do it on a tight budget, so we had to be very resourceful. Fortunately, the original house had good walls, requiring no reinforcement or insulation. Although it takes some time to heat up, the heating works well and the house is equally comfortable in winter and summer. I avoided superfluous ornamentation, steering clear of anything affected or prissy. I wanted a genuine home, easy to live in, comfortable–a country house. My obsession, I repeat, was to preserve its original character. The luxury was in its large spaces and its unpretentious sophistication.

The entrance hall, with its oak doors and the terra-cotta floor I bought near Marseilles, connects the old and new buildings. To one side, in the original house, are the kitchen area, dining room, and bedrooms. To the other, in the huge new section, are the living room, the guest bedroom and bathroom, and the common areas, including a second kitchen and a spacious playroom.

The entrance hall is decorated with some of my favorite collectibles: demijohns, or *damajuanas*, as we call them in Spain, from Eastern Europe for storing olive oil; wicker baskets, another of my weaknesses; and yes, some stuffed pheasants in honor of the farm that once was home to 30,000 birds. The two eighteenth-century stools are very French, yet rough and rustic. I bought a lot of the furniture in antiques shops and markets in the Biarritz area. Even before I acquired the house, I was keeping my eye out for furniture with the space I imagined in mind.

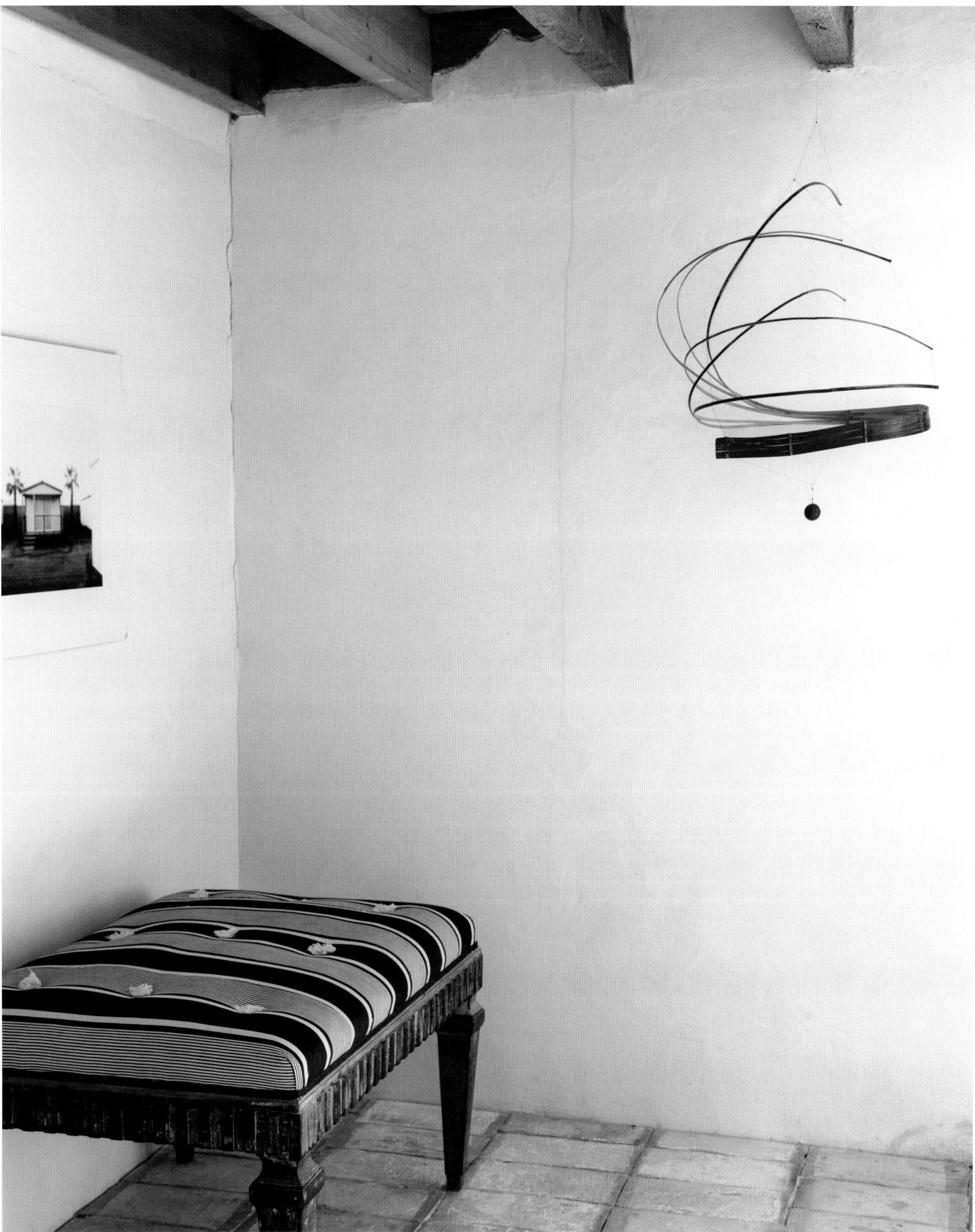

## Living Room

The enormous living room (more than 100 square meters, or 1,100 square feet) is conceived as a large pavilion. Following the natural slope of the terrain, it faces west, affording spectacular views and magnificent sunsets. The huge iron-framed glass doors are German and, owing to their size, essentially constitute a glass wall that blurs the line between indoors and outdoors. The furnishings, covered in linen, velvet, and a rich variety of printed fabrics, include a sofa that's more than 4 meters (13 feet) long, armchairs, a pair of chaises longues, and an array of pillows. Vintage American ceramic kitchen jars, topped with cobalt blue Victorian Christmas balls, are grouped on a console, adding colorful notes to the large, fresh, simple space.

I acquired the floor in London. It is made out of shelves from an old porcelain factory that I found out about by chance on a visit to England. While driving me to my hotel, my cabdriver told me the crazy story of this factory and I instantly decided to check it out, compelled by instinct and curiosity. The bookcase under the stairs is also English, though I found it in Madrid. It is in fact shelving from a little grocery store in the Salamanca district, one of the capital's most stately and traditional neighborhoods. When a friend told me that the old store was closing, I ran over and bought its entire contents. I have used many of its furnishings and fittings in a number of houses. It is funny how often I configure my spaces around these marvels I keep finding and buying by pure chance. The design of the living room's Ibiza-style double stair, for example, was directly prompted by the need to create a place for that fabulous bookcase from the store, and it turned out to be one of the most special corners of the house, devoted to books, reading, and intimate conversations.

THE ARTS IN LATIN AMERICA
1492–1820
Côte basque
Cote basque
JARDINS ET INTÉRIEURS DU
PAYS BASQUE

NEW YORK
Marella Agnelli The Last Swan
The Gardener's Garden

THE ARTS IN LATIN AMERICA
1492–1820
BASQUE

jardín en casa
ANTOLOGIA DE ESPAÑA
ESPAÑA HISTORIA GRAFICA DEL SIGLO XX
32nd AMERICA'S CUP
cocina

THE ARTS IN LATIN AMERICA
1492–1820
PAYS BASQUE
JARDINS ET INTERIEURS DU
Côte basque

Las grandes dinastías
LA CHICA DEL TREN

3
2
2

## Dining Room

The main dining room, next to the kitchen, opens up to the pergola in the garden. The simple white room features hardwood furnishings, a fireplace, and two mirrors, which increase both depth and light. We use the dining room only when we have a full house or for summer dinners. During the rest of the year, if there are no more than eight of us, we tend to use the table in the kitchen.

The dining table is Italian and stretches 4 meters (13 feet) when fully extended, but its special feature is its 1.6-meter (5 1/4-foot) width, allowing three people to be seated at each end. The 1970s black-lacquered chairs are from my parents-in-law; the green glass demijohns add color as well as another opportunity for me to play around with transparency. The two French chests, also inherited from my in-laws, and the eighteenth-century Swedish grandfather clock complete the sober, restrained look I was going for.

## Family Rooms

The kitchen gets the morning light, so welcome at breakfast time. Two huge refrigerators allow me to store enough food when we have a full house. The scullery and the kitchen also open up to the garden pergola. I furnished the kitchen in an old-fashioned way, with baskets, wooden benches, and cabinets to organize all the tableware and cutlery. In Biarritz, I have more time to go grocery shopping than in Madrid. The market is packed with the highest-quality produce, making it a real treat to shop there. With a wink at pomposity, I hung some of our ancestors' portraits in the kitchen. The ironing room, next to the kitchen and opening onto the kitchen patio, also has furnishings recycled from the old grocery store in Madrid.

In the new addition there is another, smaller kitchen, something like a large pantry, which services the veranda, the living room, and the swimming pool. It has cabinets to store beverage and aperitif glasses, as well as ceramics by the artist Gloria García Lorca, and a small Louis XVI Provençal sofa. Next to it is the playroom, furnished with a Ping-Pong table. We practice yoga there, and it also comes in handy as a spare dining room when we have a lot of guests. On such occasions, the Ping-Pong table serves as a large buffet table. This is just one example of how flexible the house is. Its versatile spaces can be repurposed, depending on the number of visitors we have.

GARANTI
GARANTI

AERIN
GARDENIA
RATTAN

## Stair Hall

The stair hall facilitates circulation in the house. It leads to the kitchen, the ironing room, the guest bathroom, and the "mud room" area for coats, hats, umbrellas, baskets, and rain boots (the grounds beckon us to take walks, rain or shine!). Facing the coat hooks is a pair of black tables where objects of all kinds pile up: a collection of white corals, Japanese prints that I brought back from Tokyo when I worked on the Spanish Embassy there, a white 1970s lamp. Like the porcelain birds found all over the house, this is one of those mixtures of objects in different styles and evoking fond memories that I enjoy having around me.

The staircase leads to the rooms on the second and third floors of the original building. Like many of the doors and much of the furniture in the house, the stair is made of oak, Its delicate, clean design is deliberately understated, almost as if it were a staircase in a simple barn.

TRABAJA
PARA TI
Editions
FLEUVE NOIR

MUJERES IMAGINADAS en Buenos Aires

# Private Rooms

## Master Bedroom

The master bedroom and our daughters' bedrooms are on the second floor of the original house. The access to the master bedroom is through a bathroom–dressing room. Farmhouses have no closets, so we had to put freestanding wardrobes in each room, and mine are in the bathroom. The first thing one sees upon entering, standing in the middle like an island, is a piece of furniture from a French café in which I installed the washbasins. Its size and personality defined the rest of the space, which is light and bright. Between the washbasins and the window is the bathtub, a fantastic design by the Australian Marc Newson.

The bedroom itself, which looks out in several directions, is predominantly white, from the bedding to the window frames and the walls, on which I left visible the scars that give the house its character. Instead of ordinary nightstands, I flanked the bed with my grandmother Isabel's old kitchen table on one side and a Carlos IV bureau inherited from my parents-in-law on the other. Porcelain birds, flowers, and books fill our most intimate room with life and color.

ETHAN CANIN AMERICA, AMÉRICA
El Jardinero Losada
Stendhal

## Children's Bedrooms

My three children's bedrooms are designed so that they can invite friends or cousins to stay with them. My son, Álvaro's room is in the attic, and he has his own bathroom. Next to the double sink is a fantastic canvas wardrobe that looks almost like a toy. My eldest, Claudia's room features an eighteenth-century Swedish corner unit, still covered in its original paint. My youngest, Isabel's room also has a corner unit. Hers is of French origin. She loves shells so much that she has two mirrors with shell-encrusted frames.

The three rooms are warm in winter and cool in summer. The palette of the walls in all of them is very soft–white or gray–and once again the touches of color come from the details: the mohair blankets, the linens from Transylvania, the embroidered bedspreads, the portrait of their grandfather Carlos, who is responsible for our being in Biarritz, and the wood, which covers the walls of one of the bathrooms almost completely.

6
6
4

## Guest Bedroom

The guest bedroom is special. When Fernando Caruncho designed the infinity pool, we thought long and hard about which room should overlook it. In the end, I decided it would be the guest room, which will in time be my husband's and mine, as it is essentially a small apartment, independent from the rest of the house.

But what is most special about the room is that a balcony opens off the window, allowing one to dive into the pool virtually from the bed. Not only is there water at the foot of the bed, but there is also the view of the horizon, the whole countryside, and the sky to enjoy while lying in bed. A genuine spectacle.

# Garden Rooms

Fernando Caruncho often says that our houses adhere to an ancient code, very Mediterranean and European, and that is why all my gardens–urban or rural–have common elements. One day Fernando admitted that he had lacked the imagination to see what I saw in the house in Biarritz, just as I had seen the potential in the old wax factory in Madrid. He helped me shape both houses through the landscaping. In Biarritz, despite all the work involved, we achieved a look that appears natural and effortless. Like the interior, it seems as if it has always been that way.

The grounds of the ten-acre farm consist of green, rolling hills. As Fernando says, you make the landscape your own "by means of the light and the sky." This garden might at first seem quite static, but when you live here and walk around in it, you discover that it is in fact very dynamic. It is a garden not only to look at but also to stroll through.

## Veranda and Pergola

The house has several outdoor seating areas. The grapevine-covered pergola is the transition between the garden and the kitchen and dining room. The veranda, located next to the swimming pool and the guest room, serves as an extension of the living room. Sheltered from the rain and sun, it offers protection no matter what the weather. Once spring arrives, we use both the pergola and the veranda constantly, day and night.

I bought the slate for the floor of the veranda from an oyster farm. Like the terra-cotta for the hall floor and the wood for the living room floor, it's a material that originally had a different purpose. My love of fabrics and vintage, weathered furniture is once again on view in the pergola. On the veranda, what appears to be a cage is in fact a model from a French carpenter's workshop, the doors are from a stable, the two tables are from an old bakery, and the wingback rattan chair is a design by Gio Ponti. Wooden tables, teak benches, wicker chairs, ceramics, baskets, flowerpots . . . In less than a decade the garden has grown so much that the furniture and vegetation are engaged in a competition for prominence.

## Kitchen Patio

The kitchen patio, accessible from the pergola and from the kitchen and the ironing room, is a sheltered place to eat breakfast or lunch outdoors when the wind whips up in the valley. Here is where I grow my aromatic cooking herbs–thyme, rosemary, and others–and my roses. The pebbled cement floor gives it that traditional patio appearance.

Next to a shed for storing firewood is my flower atelier, where I installed two genuine florist worktables on wheels, one blue and the other white. This is where I keep my pots and tools, and happily work away. I admit that working in the garden gives meaning to my life when I'm in the country. On cloudy days, I can spend hours pruning, cutting, and planting, and I love it. The oakleaf hydrangea, the leadwort, the grapevines, and the ivy all grow so much that it becomes difficult to keep the garden in check. It is a never-ending job and Tony, our gardener, takes care of everything magnificently. Helping him out with the garden tasks during vacations gives me great pleasure.

FRUITVEILING ST. TRUIDEN T.73901
1962

# Gallinero

Building the cabin, or *gallinero* (henhouse), was a wonderful adventure. Having an extra house gives us a great excuse to keep the farm full of people–my children and their friends, my siblings and their families. The second house also lets us open our doors to lots of friends. Absolutely everything was done using recycled materials, gifts from friends who are antiques dealers, and spare pieces from other houses. I love to hang on to things and make the most of them, with all that that implies: circular economy, the love of things, and respect for the environment.

In addition, the cabin's location made it possible to create the double entrance that justifies the garden path in the shade of the linden trees that creates the "dynamic effect" Fernando Caruncho talked about. "In the garden, the geometry is a receptacle of light, a wave that must be set in motion," he says.

The cabin is clad in wood and each bedroom opens out onto one of its two verandas, one to the north and the other to the south. We could be in Bali, or Montana, or the Atacama Desert because the cabin belongs to a thousand places and to none. Each room has its own personality, and I experimented with styles and layouts: one can go from room to room from the outside, and there's also a common interior corridor; everything is open yet intimate at the same time. The charming kitchen, the shower in homage to Richard Serra, the sloped ceilings, the walls covered with corrugated-metal plates, the blue shutters, the leather armchairs, the oversize coffee table topped with an Argentine rug, the vibrant colors, the exotic fabrics–there is something unreal about it, almost toylike, and happiness fills the air. It is a treasure, and I am extremely proud of it.

Papaver laciniatum rubum
Tordilion Creticum

# GRACIAS

Every day I am grateful to God for everything life has given me. ¶ I give thanks to my husband of thirty years for always being there, like a rock, for looking after our children when I have been absent, for supporting me; it is thanks to him that I have been able to do so much, to travel . . . ¶ Thanks to my three children, my three great loves, for being who they are, for filling our houses and gardens with happiness and joy. That is exactly what gives our homes their importance and meaning! I hope you fill Biarritz with grandchildren . . . ¶ I am thankful for the gift I was given, for being able to work in this fascinating profession, and for having the strength and tenacity to practice it. ¶ Thanks to my López-Quesada Sanchiz family. First, to my beloved grandmothers, who loved me so much: my paternal grandmother and godmother, Lola, the most caring, positive matriarch in the world; and Belita, Isabel, who figures so prominently in this book, for her great taste, for how lovely she was . . . To my parents, for giving us so, so much and more, and to my six sisters and my brother for always staying connected and helping one another. ¶ Thanks to Pablo Carvajal and Fernando Caruncho—being friends and working together is the best! ¶ Thanks to Miguel Flores-Vianna and Mark Magowan for making this book possible, with patience, calm, and wisdom. And to Amy Astley for the kind words she devoted to me in her Foreword; I am deeply honored by her appreciation of my work. ¶ Thank you to the incredible women who have accompanied me throughout this process: to Carmen LQ, the sixth of my siblings, for the twenty-two years we've worked together in the studio, for everything we've achieved. To Loreto LQ, my older sister, the super stylist of this book. To Inés Urquijo, the best florist in the world, as you may have noticed. To Sofía LQ, the eighth, and youngest, sibling, for her incredible advice and for always being there, protectively, with her good taste and wise corrections. To Inés LQ, the seventh sibling and my goddaughter, for filling my houses with art and for filling my life. To Natalia Cabeza de Vaca for her support in everything, including this book. To Elsa Fernández de Santos for transcribing my words and understanding me so well. ¶ Thanks to Enriqueta and César Loachamin Guachamin for looking after us and our houses, and to Tony for taking care of La Faisanderie with so much love. ¶ Thanks to JF Garabieta for so many years of friendship, laughter, and walks. ¶ Thanks to my antiquarian friends, to my suppliers, to everyone who works with me in the studio and all who have passed through it, for all the amazing teams we have formed. ¶ And thank you to all the artisans who have worked with me to create these paradises on earth with their hands and exceptional skill.

Isabel López-Quesada

At Home: Isabel López-Quesada
First published in 2018 by The Vendome Press
Vendome is a registered trademark of The Vendome Press, LLC

VENDOME PRESS US
PO Box 566
Palm Beach, FL
33480

VENDOME PRESS UK
Worlds End Studio
132–134 Lots Road
London, SW10 0RJ

www.vendomepress.com



Distributed in North America by Abrams Books

Distributed in the United Kingdom, and the rest of the world, by Thames & Hudson

ISBN 978-0-86565-355-9

PUBLISHERS: Beatrice Vincenzini, Mark Magowan, and Francesco Venturi
EDITOR: Jacqueline Decter
PRODUCTION DIRECTOR: Jim Spivey
DESIGNER: Celia Fuller

Translated from the Spanish by Daniel Lacasta Fitzsimmons

Library of Congress Cataloging-in-Publication Data
available upon request

Printed and bound in China by 1010 Printing International Ltd.
Fifth printing

Page 1: Assembled on the whitewashed-pine table in the living room of my Madrid house are some of my favorite pieces: a giant vase, an old turtle shell, a mounted coral from the 1970s, and two colored insects encased in resin by the artist Dustin Yellin.

Pages 2–3: In the dining room of the Madrid house, the enigmatic visual poetry of Jorge Méndez Blake's seventeen-part series *Nocturnos (Xavier Villaurrutia)* contrasts with the red-lacquered English chairs and the tailored striped fabric covering the wall. The effect is as dramatic as it is fresh.

Pages 4–5: Flowers, flowers forever: On the left, a detail of an old watercolor found in a French antiques market. On the right, a hallway in the Biarritz house, seen from the veranda. A French grape-harvesting table holds a collection of green cement flowerpots. On the wall, a work by the Argentine artist Máximo González depicts a squadron of planes dropping bombs that are transformed into trees when they reach the ground. Titled *La Reforestación*, it sends a pacifist and environmentalist message.

Page 6: The hallway leads to the living room of the Biarritz house.

Page 8: This corner of my decorating studio exhibits my penchant for mixing styles, objects, and colors. The oak door is eighteenth-century French, the floor is Spanish stone, the walls are covered in an English fabric, and the limestone fireplace is French.